Copyright 2024© SHERELL FLAGG, Pretty Moody, LLC and the Pretty Moody Foundation

All rights reserved. No part of this publication may be reproduced, distributed, or transmitted in any form or by any means, including photocopying, recording, or other electronic or mechanical methods, without the prior written permission of the publisher, except in the case of brief quotations embodied in critical reviews and certain other noncommercial uses permitted by copyright law. For permission requests, write to the publisher, addressed "Attention: Permissions Coordinator," at the address below.

ISBN: 979-8-218-52794-5 (Hardcover)

Front cover image by Jo'Nia Miller

Contributors: Dawn Gordon and Shelly Norman

Book design by SHERELL FLAGG
Manufactured in the United States of America
First printing edition 2024

Publisher
Sherell A. Flagg
206 Jestan Blvd
New Castle, DE 19720

For information on bulk purchases please contact sherell@prettymoody.com

This journal is humbly dedicated to my grandmothers, Shirley Scott and Ernestine Barlow. The love they gave was unconditional and made me appreciate the smallest, most beautiful and sweetest things in life (like the butterfly). They also taught me to dream without borders, have faith beyond measure, be strong, and courageous, be unapologetic and authentically me, with love. This journal is also dedicated to my beautiful daughters, I want make sure they are always better equipped than I was, especially as they embrace their journeys of womanhood. And last but not least, to every woman living in her "second spring!" You got this!

The Pretty Moody Butterfly

Butterflies are not only beautiful, but also have mystery, symbolism and meaning and are a metaphor representing spiritual rebirth, transformation, change, hope and life.

The butterfly is a profound symbol of transformation, resilience, and renewal, making it a beautiful metaphor for the menopause journey. Just as the butterfly evolves through distinct stages—egg, caterpillar, chrysalis, and finally, its vibrant emergence—it mirrors the phases of a woman's life. Each stage carries its challenges and growth, culminating in newfound strength and beauty. This transformation reminds us that menopause, too, is not an end but a powerful transition into a freer, more authentic phase of life, where wisdom and self-discovery take flight

Butterfly Meaning and Symbolism: What Does It Mean When A Butterfly Visits You? ... It is the symbol of new beginnings, resilience, endurance, and change.

I am truly honored to introduce you to this menopause journal—something I've poured my heart into creating. As a woman who is walking through the peaks and valleys of surgical menopause, I know firsthand how isolating, overwhelming, and misunderstood this journey can be. My personal experience inspired me to launch Pretty Moody as a platform of support, education, and empowerment for women like us, navigating this transformative stage of life. Additionally, to dig deeper into my realm of serving, became a certified menopause and health and wellness coach. I want to help, inspire and impact as many women as I can!

Why a journal? Because I believe in the power of reflection and writing to heal and empower. When I was deep in the trenches of menopause, journaling became one of the tools that helped me not only process my emotions but also recognize patterns in my body and mood. It became a way for me to understand what was happening. I was able to see the changes as a part of my evolving story, not as something to fear or fight against. I wanted to share that experience with you.

This journal is more than a notebook - it's a safe space for you to unpack your experiences, write your fears, celebrate your wins, and track your physical, mental, and emotional journey. It's a place for reflection, discovery, and healing. Each page is crafted with helpful information, prompts and tools that aim to help you get more in tune with your body and emotions, all while feeling supported by a community of women who know exactly what you're going through.

I created this journal because I believe that knowledge is power and when we equip ourselves with the tools to understand and embrace our changing bodies, we reclaim our power. I want this journal to be that tool for you, something that helps you feel seen, heard, and connected as you move through this phase of life. You're not alone on this journey and my hope is that each entry you write brings you closer to feeling more empowered and confident in who you are. I am not offering medical advice, but support and resources to help better equip you.

Let's journey through this together...with grace, strength, and, of course, a little moodiness!
Love, blessings, & sisterhood,

How to Use your Journal

Again, I'm thrilled that you've chosen to use the Pretty Moody Menopause Journal as part of your journey. This journal is more than a collection of pages—it's a tool designed to empower you, help you reflect, and guide you through the ups and downs of menopause.

Here's how to make the most of your journal:

1. Start With Intention
Each time you open your journal, take a moment to ground yourself. Set an intention for your entry. Whether you're documenting how you feel, tracking symptoms, or celebrating a small win, this journal is your safe space.

2. Track Your Symptoms
One of the most powerful features of this journal is symptom tracking. Use it daily or weekly to note patterns in your mood, sleep, energy levels, or physical changes. By identifying trends, you can take proactive steps to improve your well-being.

3. Express Your Emotions
Menopause can bring a whirlwind of emotions—anger, joy, confusion, peace—it's all valid. Use the journal's prompts to pour out your thoughts without judgment. Writing helps you process emotions and see the beauty in your evolution.

4. Celebrate Small Wins
Every step forward is progress. Did you try a new remedy that worked? Or finally get a good night's sleep? Write it down! These moments remind you that you're stronger than any challenge.

5. Engage With the Prompts
The journal includes thoughtful prompts designed to help you reflect on your menopause journey and rediscover yourself. From identifying what makes you feel beautiful to exploring what calms your mind, let these prompts guide you to self-discovery.

6. Use It as a Communication Tool
Bring your journal to doctor visits or share entries with loved ones. It's a wonderful way to articulate your experience and ensure others understand what you're going through.

7. Reflect Often
Flip back through your entries regularly. See how far you've come, what's working, and what might need adjustment. Reflection is key to growth and self-awareness.

8. Make It Your Own
Add doodles, stickers, quotes, or photos. The journal is yours, and there's no right or wrong way to use it. Personalize it in a way that makes you smile every time you open it.

9. Connect With the Pretty Moody Community
Share your insights or connect with others on the same journey. Join us online for more tips, support, and sisterhood. We're here to cheer you on every step of the way.

Remember, this journal is your companion, designed with love and care to help you navigate this chapter with grace and power. Thank you for trusting Pretty Moody to be a part of your story.

Menopause
Journal Prompts

Your journal is a unique support resource, that combines coaching exercises and coping strategies to fully support you on your journey. For many of us, menopause happens at a time when we are time-
poor, juggling our career with dependents, partners, caring for parents and other responsibilities, and many menopausal women feel invisible, irrelevant, lonely and overlooked by society.

- How has my body been changing, and how do I feel about these changes?
- What emotions have I been experiencing most frequently, and how can I honor them without judgment?
- What is one positive thing I've noticed about myself during this phase of life?
- Are there any patterns I'm noticing between my lifestyle choices and how I feel?
- How can I nurture my body today? (e.g., movement, rest, nourishment)
- What thoughts have I been holding onto that I need to release?
- What activities bring me joy and help me reconnect with myself?
- What do I love about this stage of my life that I didn't expect to enjoy?
- What am I most grateful for today, even if it's a small thing?
- What's one way I can celebrate myself and my body this week?
- What is one health goal I'd like to focus on during menopause, and what small steps can I take to achieve it?
- How do I envision my life post-menopause, and what excites me about that?
- What does thriving during menopause look like for me?

Let's Talk About Menopause

PRETTY MOODY

is a community based MENOPAUSE lifestyle brand started by our founder, Sherell Flagg when she was abruptly thrown into surgical menopause during the COVID-19 pandemic in 2020. She wanted to let GOD use her to be a voice and vessel to serve in the menopause arena by living her journey out loud, educating herself along the way, and using her experience to create a safe place and a blossoming community. Pretty Moody provides resources, education, beauty and wellness products for women on their menopause journey where they can simply be themselves. PRETTY MOODY, with zero judgement.

We are affected in more ways than we imagine. There are over 80 menopause symptoms & counting

Sherell Flagg

A wife, mother, mentor, certified health and wellness coach, certified menopause coach, hairstylist with over three decades of experience in the beauty industry, award winning salon co-owner of Resh Salon & Spa and Resh Hair Care Products, co-owner of Le Diner en Blanc Wilmington, and Founder & CEO of Pretty Moody and the Pretty Moody Foundation.

DID YOU KNOW?

October has been designated as 18th as World Menopause Awareness month and October 18th is the official day. As the founder of Pretty Moody, I believe World Menopause Day is a vital moment for us to raise awareness about a phase of life that impacts every woman differently yet universally. It's a day to spotlight the challenges, celebrate the strength of women navigating this transition, and share the resources and solutions that can make this journey smoother. Menopause isn't just a health issue—it's a conversation about empowerment, understanding, and embracing this powerful stage of womanhood. Together, we can break the silence and bring more support and compassion into this experience.

WHY WE NEED TO TALK

Approx. 1.3 MILLION women enter menopause yearly in the United States alone. Studies show that by the year 2025, more than a BILLION women would have entered menopause. Yet, there is still a huge void to be filled in this arena. Not only is there a lack of education, and resources, but woman are not talking about menopause mainly due to the negative stigma that surrounds the subject and not to mention how they're affected in the WORKPLACE, HOMES, & SOCIAL LIVES. We've got some work to do Pretty's!

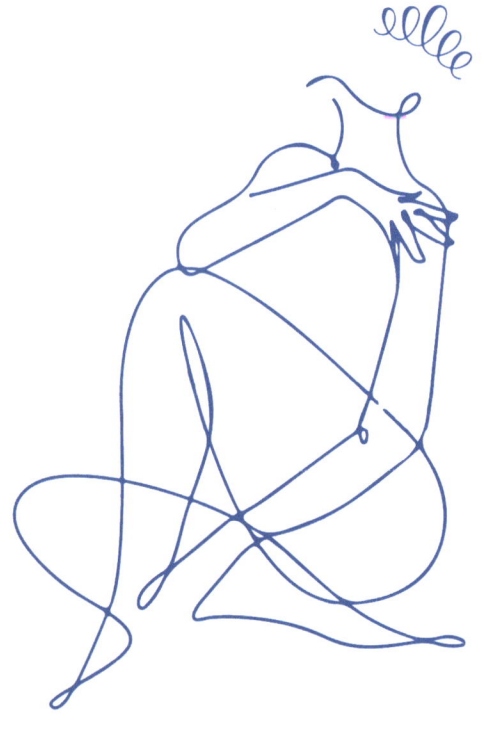

A MOVEMENT

Our mission is to educate, empower and magnify self love

What is *Menopause*

Menopause is a point in time when you've gone 12 consecutive months without a menstrual cycle. The time leading up to menopause is called pre-menopause and perimenopause. "Peri" is when a lot of women or people assigned female at birth (AFAB) start to transition to menopause. They may notice changes in their menstrual cycles or have symptoms like hot flashes, changes in sleep, mood and/or ambition. I will break down the 4 stages of menopause on the next page.

Pretty words of wisdom.. from one Pretty to another

"For me it's about being patient with yourself… Patience during menopause is an act of self-love. It's about allowing yourself time to adjust, heal, and thrive in this new chapter of life."

— D. Gordon

4 Stages of Menopause

Natural menopause is the permanent ending of menstruation that doesn't happen because of any type of medical treatment. The process is gradual and happens in four stages:

1. Pre-Menopause
the time between **MENARCHE** (a woman's first period) and the onset of perimenopause

2. Perimenopause "menopause transition"
Perimenopause can begin eight to 10 years before menopause when your ovaries gradually produce less estrogen. It usually starts when you're in your 40s, but as early as 30's. At this stage, many people may experience menopause symptoms. But, you're still having menstrual cycles during this time and can get pregnant.

3. Menopause
Menopause is the point when you no longer have menstrual periods. At this stage, your ovaries have stopped releasing eggs and stopped producing most of their estrogen. A healthcare provider diagnoses menopause when you've gone without a menstrual period for 12 consecutive months.

4. Postmenopause
This is the name given to the time after you haven't had a period for an entire year (or the rest of your life after menopause). During this stage, menopausal symptoms, such as hot flashes, may get better. However, some people continue to experience menopausal symptoms for a decade or longer after the menopause transition. As a result of a lower estrogen level, people in the postmenopausal phase are at an increased risk for several health conditions, such as osteoporosis and heart disease.

SOME SIGNS OF MENOPAUSE THAT YOU SHOULD KNOW

You may be transitioning into menopause if you begin experiencing some or all of the following symptoms: (Keep in mind, there are over 80 symptoms of menopause and counting!)

- ☐ Hot flashes also known as vasomotor symptoms (a sudden feeling of warmth that spreads over your body)
- ☐ Night sweats and/or cold flashes
- ☐ Vaginal dryness that causes discomfort during sex
- ☐ Urinary urgency (a pressing need to pee more frequently)
- ☐ Difficulty sleeping (insomnia)
- ☐ Emotional changes (irritability, mood swings or mild depression)
- ☐ Dry skin, dry eyes or dry mouth
- ☐ Breast tenderness
- ☐ Brain fog, forgetfulness
- ☐ Irregular periods or periods that are heavier or lighter than usual, Worsening of premenstrual syndrome (PMS)

Your Menopause Story
let's put it on paper

When did your journey begin?

How do you feel about your menopause? Are you excited, anxious, or scared?

What are your top menopause symptoms? How do they impact your daily life?

What self-care practices have you found helpful in managing menopause symptoms?

Have your relationships with others been affected by menopause? If yes, please explain.

What are you looking forward to in the next phase of your life?

Make An Appointment
& Talk With Your Doctor

If you think you might be experiencing symptoms of menopause, it's time to have a talk with your doctor/health care provider. They can help confirm whether menopause is the cause of your symptoms and recommend a treatment plan to fit your lifestyle preference. **The best time to talk with your doctor about menopause is early and often.**

Show up prepared - have your questions ready, write them down...you know how our meno-brain serves us.

Track your symptoms and if you have found what triggers them, so you can discuss with your doctor.

Don't be shy...remember you need answers, communicate your concerns.

ADVOCATE FOR YOURSELF.

Write down any and all info you receive.

Keep in mind, if you are **NOT** getting the satisfaction or answers that serve you, find another doctor, and another, and another until **YOU** are happy! THIS IS YOUR JOURNEY, YOUR LIFE, YOUR HEALTH. **DON'T SETTLE!**

Questions To Ask Your Doctor
About Menopause

- What are the symptoms of menopause that I might develop?
- How does my ethnic background affect my menopause symptoms?
- What should I do if I develop new or worse symptoms?
- What are the potential causes of my current symptoms?
- Could they be caused by menopause or another condition?
- Do I need to receive any tests to check for potential causes?
- What do those tests involve and how much do they cost?
- What steps can I take to manage my symptoms?
- Are there lifestyle changes that I can make to manage my symptoms?
- Are there medications or other treatments available to my manage symptoms?
- What are the potential benefits, risks, and cost of each treatment approach?
- How long should it take for the treatment to work?
- What should I do if it doesn't work?
- What are the potential side effects of treatment?
- What should I do if I develop side effects?
- How can I protect my bone health?
- Should I undergo bone density screening?
- When and how often?
- Should I get my calcium and vitamin D levels checked?
- How can I make sure that I'm getting enough calcium and vitamin D?
- Do I need to do more weight-bearing exercise to protect my bones?
- What types of activities count as weight-bearing exercise?
- Should I see a bone specialist?
- Are there other steps I can take to manage menopause and stay healthy as I get older?

Doctor Appointment
Notes

My latest period date:

Description:

Number of pregnancies:

Pregnancies historical:

Birth control use:

Side effects:

Surgeries:

Medications record :

Side effects:

Menopause symptoms experienced:

Questions To Ask My Doctor
About My Menopause

Questions to ask:

Notes:

Questions To Ask My Doctor
About My Menopause

Questions to ask:

Notes:

Questions To Ask My Doctor
About My Menopause

Questions to ask:

Notes:

Coping with Menopause Symptoms

Sometimes the menopause has no impact and people can sail through it with barely a symptom. But this transitional period is not easy for all, especially black women and women of color. Our symptoms are come earlier we are are 50% more likely to experience symptoms. They are also more severe for our ethnic backgrounds.

There are often embarrassing and stressful symptoms to contend with, which can be made worse by the negative perception of menopause in wider society, as well as a lack of resources, education and accurate knowledge regarding the subject.

Don't Suffer in Silence

Too often, people feel the need to hide their symptoms or pretend that everything is fine, when it's not. On some days, your symptoms may be manageable. But there may be other times when they become severe and you struggle to cope.

Take Control

It may not be possible to combat every symptom of menopause. But making some simple changes to your lifestyle, such as diet and exercise.

At Work - Talk to Your Manager

You may be embarrassed to broach the subject of menopause with your manager. But if you're worried that your symptoms are worsening or that they're impacting your work, then at some point you will need to talk to them about it.

This may feel particularly challenging if your boss is male. But if you have a good relationship and you can trust them, the likelihood is they will be happy to listen to your concerns and provide support.

Share Your Experience

It's important to know that you're not alone. While each person's experience will be slightly different, chances are that your co-workers even your managers! - are encountering similar challenges, too.

Managing Menopause

There are many ways to manage menopause. It may take time to find a strategy that works for you. Lifestyle changes you can implement are:

EAT HEALTHY FOOD AND DRINK LOTS OF WATER

Consuming phytoestrogens and healthy fats, such as omega-3 fatty acids from fish which can help you control your weight and reduce the risk of chronic conditions. As we get older, beginning at about age 20, the amount of water in our bodies can decrease.

DO REGULAR PHYSICAL ACTIVITY

I know it's not easy sometimes to get motivated in menopause but we should try to aim for two hours and 30 minutes of moderate aerobic activity each week. Other deep breathing, yoga, and stretching exercises can help to manage the stress of menopause life.

USE LUBRICANT

Lubrication plays an essential role in managing vaginal dryness, one of the most common symptoms of menopause. As estrogen levels decline during menopause, the vaginal tissues can become thinner, drier, and less elastic, leading to discomfort, irritation, and painful intercourse (dyspareunia). Lubricants and moisturizers help alleviate these issues, improving comfort and sexual well-being.

IMPROVE YOUR SLEEP

Mood changes, night sweats, and anxiety also will keep some women up at night, counting sheep. Not getting enough sleep can affect all areas of life. Lack of sleep can make you feel irritable or depressed, might cause you to be more forgetful than normal, which we already deal with bouts of BRAIN FOG in meno. Set a sleep routine that works for you. You may like a nice cup of tea, breathing exercises, or soothing sounds. Remember that exercise promotes healthy sleep as well.

REDUCE OR STOP UNHEALTHY HABITS

Symptoms intensify with smoking and drinking. You will more than likely experience worse hot flashes and difficulty sleeping. Stopping the use of tobacco products is one of the best things you can do for your health and will have immediate positive effects. Within 48 hours carbon monoxide is removed from the body and your oxygen supply improves significantly. You will find you have more energy, fewer mood swings and are able to cope with anxiety better.

TAKE CARE OF YOUR EMOTIONAL/MENTAL HEALTH

It's normal to experience different emotions around the time of menopause. There are many ways to take care of your emotional and mental health.

For example, having a healthy lifestyle and taking time to do things you enjoy. TALK to your friends and loved ones about what you're experiencing. This is new for you, as well as them. You can also talk to a life coach that specializes in menopause (which I am), a therapist (which I LOVE to do), or try cognitive behavioral therapy (CBT) to help manage your symptoms and emotional wellbeing.

Menopause

Menopause is our "second spring" in the asian culture. It's a time to reintroduce ourselves to this new woman we are evolving into. Embrace her, treat her well and fall in LOVE with her. Remember….she LOVES YOU!

— Sherell Flagg

Some tools to manage *Stress*

Managing stress during menopause requires a holistic approach that includes mindfulness, exercise, proper nutrition, self-care, and emotional support. By incorporating these strategies into your daily routine, you can effectively reduce stress, improve your mood, and enhance your overall well-being during this significant life transition.

Exercise Regularly
Physical activity is one of the most effective ways to reduce stress. It releases endorphins, which are natural mood boosters, and helps regulate stress hormones like cortisol.
Recommended exercises:
- Yoga: Combines physical movement with breathwork and mindfulness to reduce stress and promote emotional balance.
- Walking or hiking: Gentle aerobic exercises that provide both physical and mental relaxation.
- Strength training: Helps reduce tension and improves overall strength and bone health, which is important during menopause.

Cognitive Behavioral Therapy (CBT)
CBT is a practical approach to identifying negative thought patterns that contribute to stress and anxiety. It teaches coping strategies to handle stress more effectively.
- How it works: CBT helps you recognize and change thought patterns that lead to stress, replacing them with healthier, more constructive ways of thinking.

Practice Mindfulness and Meditation
Mindfulness helps ground you in the present moment and reduces the tendency to ruminate on negative thoughts or stressors. Meditation helps regulate emotions and calm the mind.
How to practice:
Start with 5-10 minutes of mindfulness meditation each day, focusing on your breathing or using a guided meditation app.

Journaling
Writing down your thoughts and feelings can help release emotional tension and give you a clearer perspective on stressful situations. Journaling can also help identify patterns or triggers for stress, allowing you to address them more effectively.
Tips:
- Keep a gratitude journal to focus on the positive aspects of your life.
- Write freely about your feelings to release pent-up emotions.

> "Make taking time for you a priority and Self care is imperative. I go the gym 3-4 times a week, have my bath every Wednesday night and have a massage every Friday.. it's a chair massage at the gym but it feels great and I look forward to it."
>
> —S. Rice

Pretty_words of wisdom...from one Pretty_to another

Menopause Symptoms list

just to name a few...yup, a few.

Mood swings	Vaginal dryness	Hot flashes
Fatigue	Headaches	Joint pain
Breast tenderness	Decreased libido	Irregular periods
Night sweats	Anxiety	Heart Palpitations
Brain fog	Itchiness/Dry Skin	Weight gain
Bloating	Burning mouth	Difficulty concentrating
Urinary Incontinence	Bladder infection	Body Odor
Social Withdrawal	Dizziness	Sleep Problems
Depression	Tinnitus (ear-ringing)	Nausea

Natural Remedies

Navigating menopause can feel overwhelming, but nature provides an array of herbal supplements that may help ease your symptoms. Below are some highly effective herbs and their benefits:

Black Cohosh
Why it helps:
Black Cohosh is known for its ability to reduce hot flashes and night sweats, two of the most common symptoms of menopause.
How it works:
It interacts with serotonin receptors, which play a role in body temperature regulation.

Red Clover
Why it helps:
Rich in phytoestrogens, Red Clover mimics estrogen in the body, helping balance hormone levels.
How it works:
It can alleviate hot flashes, improve bone health, and support cardiovascular health.
Image: Purple-red clover blossoms in a meadow.

Evening Primrose Oil
Why it helps:
This oil is packed with gamma-linolenic acid (GLA), which may help reduce breast tenderness and improve mood swings.
How it works:
It supports hormone production and reduces inflammation.
Image: Yellow evening primrose flowers in bloom.

Ashwagandha
Why it helps:
Ashwagandha is an adaptogen that helps manage stress, reduce anxiety, and improve sleep quality.
How it works:
It balances cortisol levels, promoting relaxation and hormonal harmony.
Image: A leafy green shrub with small red berries.

Maca Root
Why it helps:
Maca Root is celebrated for boosting energy, improving libido, and reducing hot flashes.
How it works:
It supports the endocrine system, aiding in hormone regulation.
Image: A pile of dried maca roots beside green leaves.

- Which herbal remedies or supplements have I tried recently, and how have they impacted my symptoms?
- What new natural remedies would I like to explore and why?
- How does incorporating herbs or supplements into my routine make me feel emotionally and physically?

Always consult with your health care provider

Natural Remedies

Dong Quai
Why it helps:
Often called the "female ginseng," Dong Quai improves circulation and reduces menstrual-like cramps often felt during perimenopause.
How it works:
It acts as a natural hormone balancer and anti-inflammatory agent.

Valerian Root
Why it helps:
Valerian Root promotes deep, restorative sleep and eases irritability.
How it works:
It increases GABA (gamma-aminobutyric acid) levels in the brain, creating a calming effect.

GABA (Gamma-Aminobutyric Acid)
Why it helps:
GABA is a naturally occurring neurotransmitter that calms the brain and reduces stress.
How it works:
It promotes relaxation, improves sleep quality, and reduces irritability often experienced during menopause.

Biotin
Biotin, often called vitamin B7 or vitamin H, is a water-soluble B vitamin that plays a crucial role in maintaining healthy skin, hair, and nails, as well as supporting metabolic and nervous system health. During menopause, when hormonal changes can affect many aspects of your body, biotin can offer specific benefits:

Supports Hair Health
Hormonal fluctuations during menopause often lead to thinning hair or hair loss. Estrogen, which declines during menopause, plays a role in maintaining the hair growth cycle.
How: Biotin promotes keratin production, which strengthens hair strands and may reduce breakage. It also supports hair growth and improves overall hair health, making it a popular choice for women experiencing menopausal hair changes.

Strengthens Nails
Brittle or weak nails are common during menopause due to hormonal imbalances and nutrient absorption changes.
How: Biotin strengthens the nail matrix and can improve nail thickness and resilience, reducing splitting or breakage.

Improves Skin Health
Skin can become drier and less elastic during menopause as collagen production decreases.
How: While biotin primarily supports skin hydration indirectly by aiding in fat metabolism, it may also help maintain skin barrier health, reducing dryness and irritation.

Boosts Energy and Metabolism
Menopause can bring on fatigue and sluggish metabolism. Biotin plays a role in converting food into energy by aiding the metabolism of carbohydrates, fats, and proteins.
How: Adequate biotin levels help support energy production, which can combat feelings of lethargy often associated with menopause.

Dietary Sources: Foods rich in biotin include eggs, nuts, seeds, salmon, sweet potatoes, and leafy greens.

Always consult with your health care provider

Natural Remedies
Magnesium
The Essential Mineral for Menopause

Magnesium is a powerhouse mineral with a variety of benefits for menopause symptoms. Here's how different types of magnesium can help:

Magnesium Glycinate
Why it helps:
This highly absorbable form of magnesium is excellent for calming the nervous system and improving sleep quality.
How it works:
It reduces anxiety and helps regulate melatonin production, promoting restful sleep.

Magnesium Chloride
Why it helps:
Magnesium Chloride Magnesium chloride is often referred to as "master magnesium compound," is a form of magnesium that offers various potential health benefits, both when taken orally or applied topically. Magnesium is an essential mineral involved in over 300 biochemical reactions in the body.
How it works:
Enhancing relaxation and sleep, soothing muscles and Aiding Recovery, helping alleviate depression and anxiety, relieving headaches, supporting skin health, boosting energy and endurance.
- Magnesium chloride can help replenish low levels of magnesium in the body.
- Magnesium absorption can decrease with age, making older adults more susceptible to deficiency.

Magnesium L-Threonate
Why it helps:
Known for its brain-boosting properties, this form enhances cognitive function and reduces brain fog.
How it works:
It crosses the blood-brain barrier, directly supporting memory and focus.

Magnesium Malate
Why it helps:
This type combats fatigue and boosts energy levels, which can dip during menopause.
How it works:
It supports cellular energy production by aiding in ATP (adenosine triphosphate) synthesis.

Magnesium Oxide
Why it helps:
While less bioavailable, Magnesium Oxide is effective for relieving headaches and muscle cramps.
How it works:
It provides a quick magnesium boost to alleviate physical tension.

Why Magnesium is Essential During Menopause
- Balances Hormones: Helps regulate stress hormones like cortisol.
- Eases Hot Flashes: Supports the hypothalamus, the part of the brain responsible for temperature regulation.
- Supports Bone Health: Essential for calcium absorption and maintaining bone density.
- Reduces Mood Swings: Promotes serotonin production, improving mood stability

Always consult with your health care provider

Menopause
Symptom Tracker

Symptoms	How often I experience this symptoms			Details
	Never	Sometimes	Regularly	
Vaginal dryness				
Mood swings				
Hot flashes				
Fatigue				
Headaches				
Joint pain				
Breast tenderness				
Decreased libido				
Irregular periods				
Night sweats				
Anxiety				
Palpitations				
Brain fog				
Itchiness				
Weight gain				
Bloating				
Burning mouth				
Bladder infection				
Difficulty concentrating				
Body odour				
Depression				
Dizziness				
Electric shock sensations				
Bladder weakness				

Menopause
Symptom Tracker

Symptoms being tracked:

Week beginning date:

	MORNING	EVENING	NIGHT
SUNDAY			
MONDAY			
TUESDAY			
WEDNESDAY			
THURSDAY			
FRIDAY			
SATURDAY			

Notes:

Menopause
Symptom Tracker

Symptoms being tracked:

Week beginning date:

	MORNING	EVENING	NIGHT
SUNDAY			
MONDAY			
TUESDAY			
WEDNESDAY			
THURSDAY			
FRIDAY			
SATURDAY			

Notes:

Menopause

Symptoms being tracked:

Week beginning date:

	MORNING	EVENING	NIGHT
SUNDAY			
MONDAY			
TUESDAY			
WEDNESDAY			
THURSDAY			
FRIDAY			
SATURDAY			

Notes:

Menopause
Symptom Tracker

Month: _____

Symptoms	1	2	3	4	5	6	7	8	9	10	11	12	13	14	15	16	17	18	19	20	21	22	23	24	25	26	27	28	29	30	31
Vaginal dryness																															
Mood swings																															
Hot flashes																															
Fatigue																															
Headaches																															
Joint pain																															
Breast tenderness																															
Decreased libido																															
Irregular periods																															
Night sweats																															
Anxiety																															
Palpitations																															
Brain fog																															
Itchiness																															
Weight gain																															
Bloating																															
Burning mouth																															
Bladder infection																															
Difficulty concentrating																															
Body odour																															
Depression																															
Dizziness																															
Electric shock sensations																															
Bladder weakness																															

Notes

Symptoms Tracker

Month: _____

Sun	Mon	Tue	Wed	Thu	Fri	Sat
Score:	Score:	Score:	Score:	Score:	Score:	Score:
Score:	Score:	Score:	Score:	Score:	Score:	Score:
Score:	Score:	Score:	Score:	Score:	Score:	Score:
Score:	Score:	Score:	Score:	Score:	Score:	Score:
Score:	Score:	Score:	Score:	Score:	Score:	Score:
Score:	Score:	Score:	Score:	Score:	Score:	Score:

1. Vaginal dryness
2. Mood swings
3. Hot flashes
4. Fatigue
5. Headaches
6. Joint pain
7. Breast tenderness
8. Decreased libido
9. Irregular periods
10. Night sweats
11. Anxiety
12. Palpitations
13. Brain fog
14. Itchiness
15. Weight gain
16. Bloating
17. Burning mouth
18. Bladder infection
19. Difficulty concentrating
20. Body odour
21. Depression
22. Dizziness
23. Electric shock sensations
24. Bladder weaknes

Symptoms Tracker

Month: _____

Sun	Mon	Tue	Wed	Thu	Fri	Sat
Score:	Score:	Score:	Score:	Score:	Score:	Score:
Score:	Score:	Score:	Score:	Score:	Score:	Score:
Score:	Score:	Score:	Score:	Score:	Score:	Score:
Score:	Score:	Score:	Score:	Score:	Score:	Score:
Score:	Score:	Score:	Score:	Score:	Score:	Score:
Score:	Score:	Score:	Score:	Score:	Score:	Score:

1. Vaginal dryness
2. Mood swings
3. Hot flashes
4. Fatigue
5. Headaches
6. Joint pain
7. Breast tenderness
8. Decreased libido
9. Irregular periods
10. Night sweats
11. Anxiety
12. Palpitations
13. Brain fog
14. Itchiness
15. Weight gain
16. Bloating
17. Burning mouth
18. Bladder infection
19. Difficulty concentrating
20. Body odour
21. Depression
22. Dizziness
23. Electric shock sensations
24. Bladder weaknes

Period

Year: _____

Month	1	2	3	4	5	6	7	8	9	10	11	12	13	14	15	16	17	18	19	20	21	22	23	24	25	26	27	28	29	30	31
January																															
February																															
March																															
April																															
May																															
June																															
July																															
August																															
September																															
October																															
November																															
December																															

Cycle Length	Key	Notes
January		
February		
March		
Aprll		
May		
June		
July		
August		
September		
October		
November		
December		

Period

Year: _____

Month	1	2	3	4	5	6	7	8	9	10	11	12	13	14	15	16	17	18	19	20	21	22	23	24	25	26	27	28	29	30	31
January																															
February																															
March																															
April																															
May																															
June																															
July																															
August																															
September																															
October																															
November																															
December																															

Cycle Length

January	
February	
March	
April	
May	
June	
July	
August	
September	
October	
November	
December	

Key

Notes

Sleep Tracker

Month: _____

	20	21	22	23	24	1	2	3	4	5	6	7	8	9	10	11	12	Good	Bad
				Sleep Duration														**How was your sleep?**	
1																			
2																			
3																			
4																			
5																			
6																			
7																			
8																			
9																			
10																			
11																			
12																			
13																			
14																			
15																			
16																			
17																			
18																			
19																			
20																			
21																			
22																			
23																			
24																			
25																			
26																			
27																			
28																			
29																			
30																			
31																			

Sleep

Month: _____

	20	21	22	23	24	1	2	3	4	5	6	7	8	9	10	11	12	13	14	15	16	17	18	19
Sleep Duration 24 Hours																									
1																								
2																								
3																								
4																								
5																								
6																								
7																								
8																								
9																								
10																								
11																								
12																								
13																								
14																								
15																								
16																								
17																								
18																								
19																								
20																								
21																								
22																								
23																								
24																								
25																								
26																								
27																								
28																								
29																								
30																								
31																								

Coping With Menopause in your *Relationships*

Relationship and Communication Prompts
- How can I communicate my needs to my loved ones more clearly?
- Who has been a strong source of support for me, and how can I express my gratitude to them?
- What boundaries do I need to set to protect my energy during this time?

How Menopause Impacts Your Relationships

Menopause isn't just a personal journey—it's a journey that can ripple into your relationships with your partner, children, friends, and colleagues. The changes we experience—hormonal, emotional, and physical—often affect how we communicate, connect, and show up for those around us. And let's be honest, these shifts can feel overwhelming at times. But they can also be an opportunity for growth and deeper intimacy if approached with love and understanding.

Here's the reality: menopause can bring irritability, mood swings, fatigue, or even a lower libido. These changes might lead to misunderstandings or distance in relationships. You might feel like a stranger in your own body at times, and that can make it hard to let others in. But here's the good news—when you take the time to honor your needs and openly communicate, you can foster relationships that are not just strong but thriving.

Tips for Thriving Relationships During Menopause

Open Up About Your Experience

Your loved ones can't support you if they don't know what's happening. Share your journey—how you're feeling, what's been hard, and what you need.

Example: "I've been feeling more tired lately because of some changes my body is going through. I'd love your patience and understanding while I navigate this."

Prioritize Self-Care

A well-nurtured you is better equipped to nurture relationships. Make time to recharge, whether through rest, exercise, or hobbies that bring you joy. Let your loved ones know that prioritizing yourself is also a gift to them.

Practice Compassion

Menopause may test your patience, and not everyone will "get it" right away. Extend grace to those around you, but also remind them that empathy goes both ways.

Pro Tip: Use "I" statements to express your feelings without assigning blame. For example, "I feel overwhelmed when I don't feel heard" instead of "You never listen."

Keep Intimacy Alive

Physical intimacy might shift during menopause, and that's okay. Explore new ways to connect—emotional intimacy, physical touch like hand-holding or cuddling, or even scheduling "us time."

If libido changes are a concern, consider natural remedies like maca or damiana, and focus on creating moments that build trust and closeness.

Educate Together

Invite your partner or loved ones to learn about menopause alongside you. When they understand what you're going through, they'll be better equipped to support you.

Set Boundaries Without Guilt

If you're feeling drained, it's okay to say no. Protecting your energy isn't selfish—it's essential for showing up as your best self.

Celebrate the New You

Embrace the wisdom and self-assuredness that comes with this stage of life. Share your victories, big or small, with those closest to you and celebrate together.

Remember, relationships are dynamic, and it's natural for them to change as we change. Menopause can feel like a storm at times, but with intention and love, you can build even stronger foundations that weather anything.

You've got this, and so do your relationships!

Coping With *Menopause* Symptoms at Work

Menopausal women are the fastest-growing demographic in the workforce and menopause can highly affect a woman's working life. Sometimes menopausal symptoms or working conditions can impact your ability to concentrate or carry out your role to the best of your ability. So it's important now more than ever to be able to speak openly about menopause at work, and reasonable adjustments be made within your workplace to help you manage your menopausal symptoms, such as:

- [ ] **Flexible working schedule**
- [ ] **Dress in layers, and peel as needed**
- [ ] **You may need to negotiate & incorporate more breaks than usual**
- [ ] **Access to mental health resources and support**
- [ ] **Moving to a cooler part of the office and/or asking for a fan**
- [ ] **Using technology where it can help you, for example setting up reminders on your phone or taking more notes to help with 'brain fog'**
- [ ] **Lead the conversation in your workplace - be the voice.**

It's useful to think about the practical changes that will help you. If you have access to an occupational health service, you can speak to them about support and possible work adjustments. PRETTY MOODY can also be booked to come into your workplace to help bridge the gaps and have those uncomfortable conversations for you.

Menopause symptoms
At Work

Am I losing confidence in skills and abilities

What would improve conditions for me as I experience menopause symptoms at work?

How can I manage proactively and positively if my performance is affected by the menopause?

Menopause symptoms
At Work

Am I losing confidence in skills and abilities

What would improve conditions for me as I experience menopause symptoms at work?

How can I manage proactively and positively if my performance is affected by the menopause?

Menopause symptoms
At Work

Am I losing confidence in skills and abilities

What would improve conditions for me as I experience menopause symptoms at work?

How can I manage proactively and positively if my performance is affected by the menopause?

Ways to Improve Mood

Practice Mindfulness

Mindfulness activities are among the many crucial tips to improve your mood.

Talk to yourself positively

Constructive self-talk, on the other hand, can help us to cope with life's difficulties. Notice what you say to yourself and work on more helpful and calming.

Go for gratitude

Gratitude can be an effective antidote when you're feeling low. Focusing on the positive aspects of your life can help you distance yourself from the negative.

Get plenty of sleep

Menopause can cause sleep disturbances as we know, and people who do not get enough sleep can experience lower moods and stress. This will bring the meno symptoms out to parer-tay! Work on a having a good sleep routine.

Journal

Writing down your thoughts and feelings can help release emotional tension and give you a clearer perspective on stressful situations. Journaling can also help identify patterns or triggers for stress, allowing you to address them more effectively.

Stay active

Exercise, even a brisk 10 minute walk, can relieve stress and release endorphins - the feel good hormones. And we all need more "feel good" in menopause.

Give back

Finding ways to help others often results in making you feel good yourself

Address stress

Try yoga, meditation, or another relaxation technique to help you de-stress and improve your mood

Talk to someone

It doesn't matter whether you meet up face to face, talk on the phone, chat online. Connecting with other people helps to if you're having a bad day, helping to brighten someone else's day may make you feel better

4 Holistic Tools
To Improve Your Mood

Holistic tools can play a vital role in improving mood during menopause by addressing the mind, body, and emotional well-being in a natural, integrated way. Menopause often brings about mood swings, irritability, anxiety, and even depression due to hormonal fluctuations, and holistic approaches offer gentle, effective strategies to manage these changes without relying solely on medication.

Positive Affirmations

Positively loaded phrases, or statements that are used to challenge unhelpful or negative thoughts. People can use positive affirmations to motivate them, encourage positive changes in their life, or boost their self-esteem

Mindfulness Meditation

Type of meditation in which you focus on being intensely aware of what you're sensing and feeling in the moment, without interpretation or judgment. Practicing mindfulness involves breathing methods, guided imagery, and other practices to relax the body and mind and help reduce stress.

Breath Work

Breathwork techniques can be highly beneficial for managing menopause symptoms like hot flashes, anxiety, and stress. These methods focus on using controlled breathing to calm the nervous system, balance hormones, and improve overall well-being.

Cognitive Reframing

Psychological technique that consists of identifying and then changing the way situations, experiences, events, ideas, and/or emotions are viewed. Cognitive reframing is the process by which such situations or thoughts are challenged and then changed.

Yoga

Yoga offers a holistic approach to managing menopause symptoms by addressing physical discomfort, emotional fluctuations, and overall well-being. The gentle, holistic approach of yoga helps balance hormones, improve mood, and promote overall well-being

The Emotions Wheel

When used as a way to check in with yourself, emotion wheels are useful tools for building self-awareness. There are two main ways that this develops emotional literacy. The first is that it makes it easier to understand and express how you're feeling. There are times when our emotions are fairly straightforward. For example, we might feel gratitude when someone does something nice for us. In those cases, a feelings wheel may be of limited use. You probably already know what the emotion is reflecting and how it impacts your behavior. This is the second primary benefit of the emotion wheel the understanding of emotion as a way of triggering survival-oriented behavior. When we think of emotions as an uncontrollable nuisance, we can't do much about them. But when we understand what they're trying to say, we can address the real need under the surface.

- What word describes your primary emotion right now?
- How would you describe that emotion?
- How does your body feel?
- Is there an event, person, place, or thing that might have caused this response?
- How did you react to that trigger?
- How will you respond now?
- Are there any emotions that I'm suppressing or not acknowledging?
- How can I express my emotions in a healthy and constructive way?
- What kind of support do I need to help me manage my emotions during menopause?

The Emotions Wheel

The Emotions Wheel, is an amazing measuring technique created by Robert Plutchik, can also be used to reflect on some of the bridges we experience between our emotions (e.g., anger and sadness may frequently co-occur). To help people regulate their emotions, the Emotion Wheel can be a visual aid for converting emotions from negative to positive (like going from sadness to serenity). Understanding the underlying functions of each emotion can also help people discuss the root causes of their feelings.

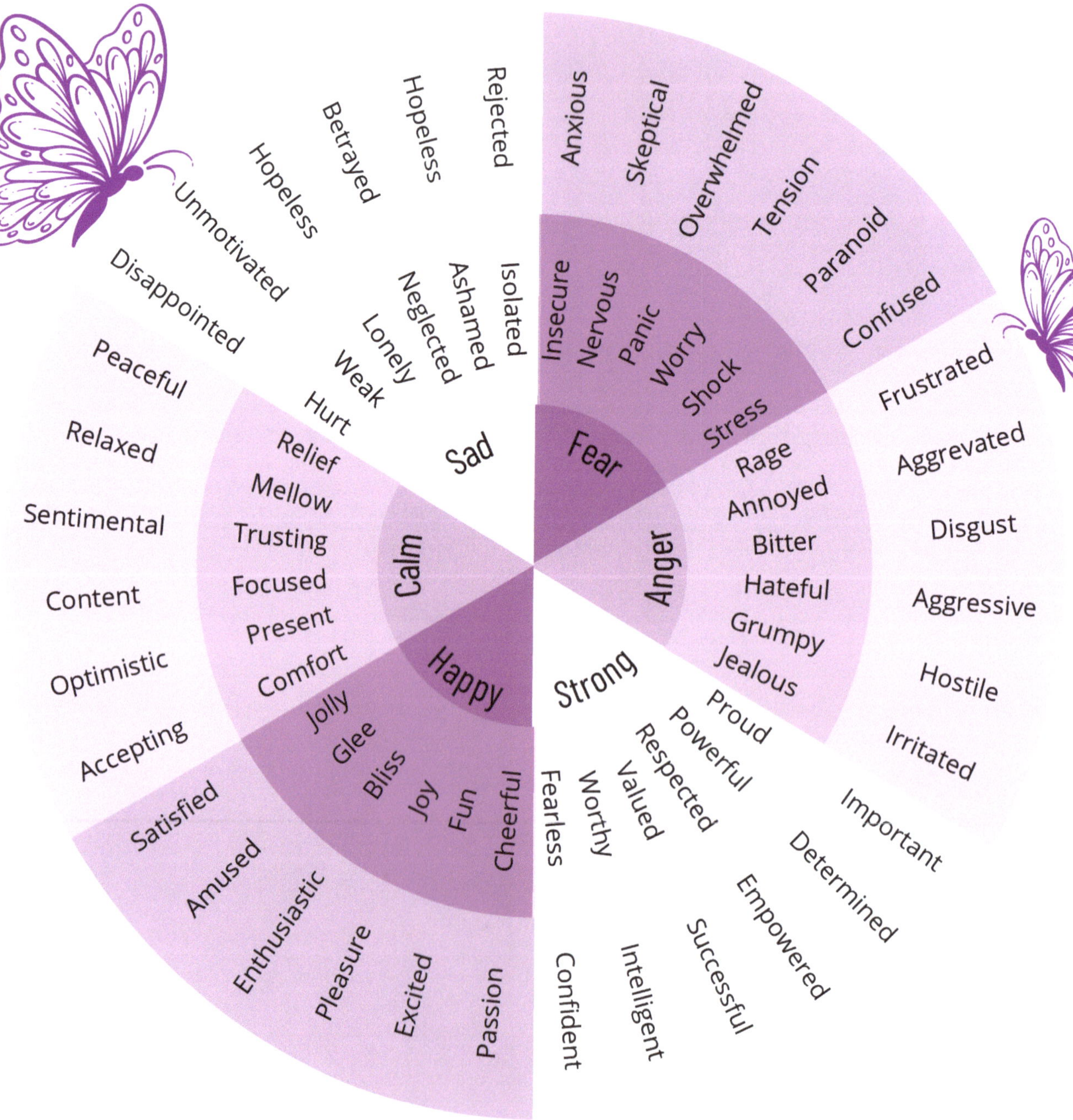

Sad
Rejected, Hopeless, Betrayed, Hopeless, Unmotivated, Disappointed, Ashamed, Neglected, Lonely, Weak, Hurt, Isolated

Fear
Anxious, Skeptical, Overwhelmed, Tension, Paranoid, Confused, Insecure, Nervous, Panic, Worry, Shock, Stress

Anger
Frustrated, Aggravated, Disgust, Aggressive, Hostile, Irritated, Rage, Annoyed, Bitter, Hateful, Grumpy, Jealous

Strong
Proud, Powerful, Respected, Valued, Worthy, Fearless, Important, Determined, Empowered, Successful, Intelligent, Confident

Happy
Cheerful, Fun, Joy, Bliss, Glee, Jolly, Passion, Excited, Pleasure, Enthusiastic, Amused, Satisfied

Calm
Relief, Mellow, Trusting, Focused, Present, Comfort, Peaceful, Relaxed, Sentimental, Content, Optimistic, Accepting

Mood Tracker

Month:

Today I Feel

1. Cheerful
2. Reflective
3. Gloomy
4. Humorous
5. Melancholy
6. Idyllic
7. Whimsical
8. Romantic
9. Mysterious
10. Ominous
11. Calm
12. Lighthearted
13. Hopeful
14. Angry
15. Fearful
16. Tense
17. Lonely

Mood Tracker

Year: _____

Month	1	2	3	4	5	6	7	8	9	10	11	12	13	14	15	16	17	18	19	20	21	22	23	24	25	26	27	28	29	30	31
January																															
February																															
March																															
April																															
May																															
June																															
July																															
August																															
September																															
October																															
November																															
December																															

Rate your mood from 1 (lowest) to 5 (highest)

Key	Review this year	Notes

Mood Tracker

Year: _____

Month	1	2	3	4	5	6	7	8	9	10	11	12	13	14	15	16	17	18	19	20	21	22	23	24	25	26	27	28	29	30	31
January																															
February																															
March																															
April																															
May																															
June																															
July																															
August																															
September																															
October																															
November																															
December																															

Rate your mood from 1 (lowest) to 5 (highest)

Key	Review this year	Notes

Mood
Diary

Month: _____ **Date:** _____ S M T W T F S

Hours	HAPPY	SAD	ANXIOUS	ANGRY	NOTES
6.00 - 8.00 AM					
8.00 - 10.00 AM					
10.00 AM - 12.00 PM					
12.00 - 2.00 PM					
2.00 - 4.00 PM					
4.00 - 6.00 PM					
6.00 - 8.00 PM					
8.00 - 10.00 PM					
10.00 PM - 12.00 AM					

Notes:

Mood

Month: **Date:**   S   M   T   W   T   F   S

Hours	HAPPY	SAD	ANXIOUS	ANGRY	NOTES
6.00 - 8.00 AM					
8.00 - 10.00 AM					
10.00 AM - 12.00 PM					
12.00 - 2.00 PM					
2.00 - 4.00 PM					
4.00 - 6.00 PM					
6.00 - 8.00 PM					
8.00 - 10.00 PM					
10.00 PM - 12.00 AM					

Notes:

Mood Diary

Month: _____ **Date:** _____ S M T W T F S

Hours	HAPPY	SAD	ANXIOUS	ANGRY	NOTES
6.00 – 8.00 AM					
8.00 – 10.00 AM					
10.00 AM – 12.00 PM					
12.00 – 2.00 PM					
2.00 – 4.00 PM					
4.00 – 6.00 PM					
6.00 – 8.00 PM					
8.00 – 10.00 PM					
10.00 PM – 12.00 AM					

Notes:

Habit
Tracker

Month: _____

	Exercise	Meditation	Healthy Food	Water	Sleep	Medication	Sweets	Alcohol
1								
2								
3								
4								
5								
6								
7								
8								
9								
10								
11								
12								
13								
14								
15								
16								
17								
18								
19								
20								
21								
22								
23								
24								
25								
26								
27								
28								
29								
30								
31								

Habit Tracker

Month:

	Exercise	Meditation	Healthy Food	Water	Sleep	Medication	Sweets	Alcohol
1								
2								
3								
4								
5								
6								
7								
8								
9								
10								
11								
12								
13								
14								
15								
16								
17								
18								
19								
20								
21								
22								
23								
24								
25								
26								
27								
28								
29								
30								
31								

Habit Tracker

Month: _____

1 2 3 4 5 6 7 8 9 10 11 12 13 14 15 16 17 18 19 20 21 22 23 24 25 26 27 28 29 30 31

Habit Tracker

Month: _____

Weight Loss Tracker

Start Date: _____

Week 1   Week 2   Week 3   Week 4

Week 5   Week 6   Week 7   Week 8

Week 9   Week 10   Week 11   Week 12

Week 13   Week 14   Week 15   Week 16

Weight Loss Tracker

Start Date: _____

Week 1

Week 2

Week 3

Week 4

Week 5

Week 6

Week 7

Week 8

Week 9

Week 10

Week 11

Week 12

Week 13

Week 14

Week 15

Week 16

Positivity Planner

Month: _____ **Date:** _____ S M T W T F S

Today, I am proud of

I love that I am

I am inspired by

I feel confident when I

Positivity Planner

Month: **Date:**   S M T W T F S

Today, I am proud of

I love that I am

I am inspired by

I feel confident when I

Positivity Planner

Month: **Date:** S M T W T F S

Today, I am proud of

I love that I am

I am inspired by

I feel confident when I

Positivity Planner

Month: _____	**Date:** _____	S M T W T F S

Today, I am proud of

I love that I am

I am inspired by

I feel confident when I

Positivity Planner

Month: _____ **Date:** _____ S M T W T F S

Today, I am grateful for

To do list

Water intake:
Fruits & Veggies:
Moods:

Meals for today

Notes

My treat today is

Positivity Planner

Month: **Date:** S M T W T F S

Today, I am grateful for

To do list

Water intake:
Fruits & Veggies:
Moods:

Meals for today

Notes

My treat today is

Positivity Planner

Month: **Date:**   S M T W T F S

Today, I am grateful for

To do list

Water intake:

Fruits & Veggies:

Moods:

Meals for today

Notes

My treat today is

Weekly Success

Month: **Week:**

What was my biggest achievement for the week?

What was my deepest impression during the week?

What did I do to keep myself fit and healthy?

How much time did I spend with my close ones?

How's this week going?

Weekly Success

Month: _____ **Week:** _____

What was my biggest achievement for the week?

What was my deepest impression during the week?

What did I do to keep myself fit and healthy?

How much time did I spend with my close ones?

How's this week going?

Weekly Success

Month: _____ **Week:** _____

What was my biggest achievement for the week?

What was my deepest impression during the week?

What did I do to keep myself fit and healthy?

How much time did I spend with my close ones?

How's this week going?

Weekly Success

Month: **Week:**

What was my biggest achievement for the week?

What was my deepest impression during the week?

What did I do to keep myself fit and healthy?

How much time did I spend with my close ones?

How's this week going?

Gratitude log

Date:

I am grateful for

Date:

I am grateful for

Date:

I am grateful for

Date:

I am grateful for

Gratitude
log

Date:

I am grateful for

Date:

I am grateful for

Date:

I am grateful for

Date:

I am grateful for

Gratitude log

Date:

I am grateful for

Date:

I am grateful for

Date:

I am grateful for

Date:

I am grateful for

Gratitude log

Date:

I am grateful for

Date:

I am grateful for

Date:

I am grateful for

Date:

I am grateful for

Gratitude Tracker

Month:

There is always Something to be grateful for

1 2 3 4 5 6 7 8 9 10 11 12 13 14 15 16 17 18 19 20 21 22 23 24 25 26 27 28 29 30 31

Notes

_____
_____
_____
_____
_____
_____
_____
_____

Day:

Month:

Woke up at:

Today's Affirmation

Today's Goal

List To Do

Today I am grateful for

What would make today great

3 Things that I am proud about today

Today I learned

Tomorrow I want to be

My thought for today:

Sleep At:

Daily Gratitude

Day:

Month:

Woke up at:

Today's Affirmation

Today's Goal

List To Do

Today I am grateful for

What would make today great

3 Things that I am proud about today

Today I learned

Tomorrow I want to be

My thought for today:

Sleep At:

Daily Gratitude

Day:

Month: ☀ **Woke up at:**

Today's Affirmation

Today's Goal

List To Do

Today I am grateful for

What would make today great

3 Things that I am proud about today

Today I learned

Tomorrow I want to be

My thought for today:

Sleep At:

Daily Gratitude

Day:

Month: **Woke up at:**

Today's Affirmation

Today's Goal

List To Do

Today I am grateful for

What would make today great

3 Things that I am proud about today

Today I learned

Tomorrow I want to be

My thought for today:

Sleep At:

Yearly Goals
Planner

January

February

March

April

May

June

July

August

September

October

November

December

Yearly Goals
Planner

January

February

March

April

May

June

July

August

September

October

November

December

My Affirmations

I embrace each day and what shows up in this time of transition.

As I face the unknown aspects in front of me, I let go of any aspects that are holding me back.

The need for control will keep me feeling stuck.

I am willing to soften and open myself to the possibilities ahead.

I am beautiful through and through; I choose to love myself.

I reach out and know I have all the resources I need.

I welcome the importance of the role that I am transitioning into.

I embody this body, even as it continues to change.

I am willing to discover parts of myself that I may have overlooked.

I create time and space to embrace what I want and need.
I am always enough.

As I prepare for a restful night sleep, I feel grateful for_____I welcome the wisdom of the women before me. I love and honor myself.

My Affirmations

01	02
03	04
05	06
07	08
09	10

My
Affirmations

01

02

03

04

05

06

07

08

09

10

Copy Right

The Pretty Moody Menopause Journal and all associated content provided by Sherell Flagg and Pretty Moody are intended for informational and educational purposes only. The journal is not a substitute for professional medical advice, diagnosis, or treatment. Always seek the advice of your physician or another qualified healthcare provider with any questions you may have regarding menopause or any other medical condition.

Sherell Flagg, Pretty Moody, and any associated parties make no claims regarding the prevention, treatment, or cure of any medical condition. The use of the Pretty Moody Menopause Journal is at the user's discretion and risk. Any decisions or actions based on the contents of the journal should be made in consultation with a healthcare professional.

By using the Pretty Moody Menopause Journal, you acknowledge that Sherell Flagg and Pretty Moody are not liable for any adverse effects or outcomes resulting from its use. Always consult a qualified healthcare provider before making any changes to your health regimen.

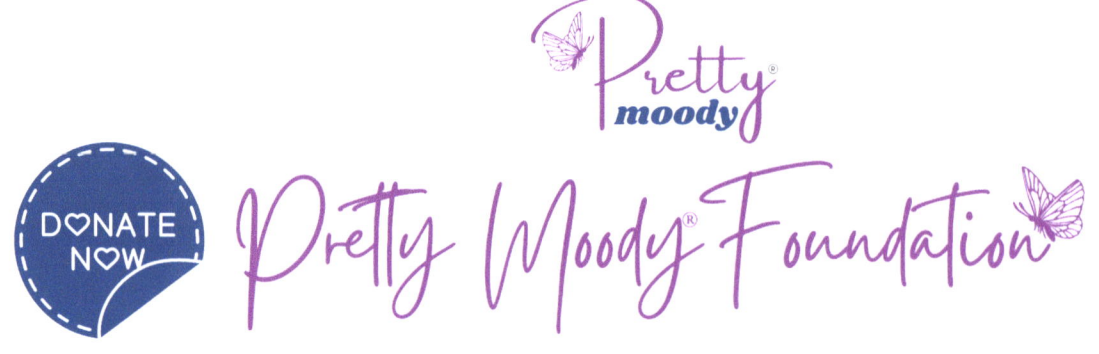

COPYRIGHT PRETTY MOODY® ALL RIGHTS RESERVED

www.prettymoody.com

www.ingramcontent.com/pod-product-compliance
Lightning Source LLC
Chambersburg PA
CBHW041417010526
44107CB00016B/1200